WHAT MONEY GURUS WON'T TELL YOU

Busting Common Money Myths

Peter Pen

Stardust

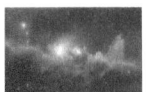

DON'T TRY TO
LOOK RICH

One of the most common mistakes that people make, is their constant effort and desire to look rich. This desire is inherent in human beings but the internet boom followed by ubiquitous use of social media has turned this disease into a pandemic. In our daily life, when we see around and meet people, we get inadvertently influenced by people's possessions. We like the new car that our neighbors have bought more than ours. We love the dress our colleague wears at the office party. We just want to have that Gucci purse that we saw on display. No matter what the price is, we yearn to buy that expensive purse at any cost. When we see our friend upgrading his cell phone, we also want to do that. We want to shift to an upscale locality like 'them'. We are envious of what people have so we want to have that too. We can look at 'have nots' of the society and be calm as that invokes our sympathy. But we just cannot look at the 'Haves' of society without admiration, envy of jealousy. In our pursuit to look richer than what we are, we end up getting poorer than what we were.

Our urge to consume brands, associate with them, love them and flash them has no ending. It's an unquenchable thirst of a person with an insatiable appetite. Interestingly, studies show that 'Brand Consciousness' is more ingrained in the minds of middle class than the wealthy people. Rather, in most cases, rich people don't care about brands. They simply choose what they are comfortable with or what looks good on them. Psychological analyses reveal that humans have inherent belief to associate wealth with success. Human beings also have a constant desire to seek attention of others and believe that wealth is one of the most effective and powerful way to invite envy of others and gain limelight. So those who are trying to look rich actually want to show others that they are successful (though they are not) and deserve their attention.

In pursuit of our struggle to look rich, we violate the most basic rule of getting rich – i.e. to control our spending. To add fuel to the fire, commercial banks have made spending so much easier for everyone through credit cards. Credit card effectively means that you can spend more than you earn. So if I have a credit card, my buying power is inflated and I have a false sense of being richer than what I am. By criticizing credit cards, I do not mean we should not keep them. In these days, of course, it is not feasible to live a life without credit cards. Instead, if used smartly with financial discipline, we can reap many benefits from credit cards as well. But the problem arises when many of us take more than one credit card, max them out and are unable to pay fully before the deadline. We then get trapped into a vicious debt which destroys our financial, social and personal life.

The urge to look rich impacts our lives in many ways. Other than jeopardizing our financial well-being, it affects our mental peace. Since we are not actually rich (we know it deep down), when we spend liberally, our mind keep reminding us of the inconvenient truth that we are treading towards bad debt. This thought makes us uncomfortable. By buying stuff which is more expensive than we can afford, we manage to get instant gratification but lose our inner peace. Moreover, efforts to copy a luxury lifestyle is an exercise in futility. You can stretch your budget to buy the tops brands. You can even manage to convince a bank finance your flashy car. But you will still find yourself wanting when it comes to expensive houses, luxury holidays, art collections bought in expensive auctions and many many more. **We must also remember that while rich people spend pittance of their income on their lifestyle, we spend a fortune to imitate them. A self-destructive struggle which makes us even poorer and divert us from the path of getting rich.**

MONEY IS MADE IN BUYING NOT SELLING

It is generally believed that we make money when we buy something of value, hold it for some time, and as the price increases, sell it high. Rich people will tell you the same logical thing. But what they will not tell you is what is most critical thing in this seemingly simple strategy. And by focusing on that (often played down) part of the deal, rich people make big money. That part of the deal is to buy an asset or equity at a much lower price than its actual value. Yes! This is where money is made. Warren Buffet built his wealth by buying value or growth stocks. The stocks whose offering price was much lower than the actual worth or earning potential of company. He bought his first stock at the age of 11 in 1942. Instead of selling out his shares during financial crises of 1987, 1990 or 2008, he capitalized on the oppurtunity and bought as many stocks as he could. When other investors were selling their stocks at cheap rates in panic, he was happily buying them at good price. His famous quote "Be greedy when others are fearful and be fearful when others are greedy" is based on his more than 40 years investment experience. If you buy crash stocks when stock exchange has nearly bottomed, you are sure to make big gains in long term. Robert Kiyosaki's success story is also based on buying under-valued real estate assets and selling them at higher rates. Even during his morning jog, he used to hunt for properties that are on sale for long. Sensing the desperate seller, he would use his negotiating skills to buy the property at much lower price than its actual value. In both above examples, we have talked about buing things than theri actual value. But here the catch lies. What is the actual value of the asset or stock is a matter of research, study and experience. That is where Money Gurus beat others. They estimate the actual value and are willing to take the risk involved. As these money moguls grow in experince, their risk appetite increases. Interestingly, most of the times, what appears a risky deal to others, appear a hot deal to them.

It is an interesting fact that despite logical reasoning behind buying assets at lower rates when markets are down, people behave entirely different when buying assets and consumables.

Take this example. You love the new model launched by Rado Watches. You are anxious to buy it but find it too expensive. After some time, the shop puts sale on the same model and now it is available at 70% of the original price. Oh Yes! You jump onto buy it. Now compare it with example of a depreciating land in your neighborhood or a crashing stock market. Although you have cash available to buy the stocks or real estate at an excellent price but you wouldn't invest in it. It's human psychology to fear from investing in a falling market despite lucrative prices for easy picking. If we analyze data of US Stock market, we come to know that people invested more money when market was high, overbought or inflated. But during the big recession slumps, people kept their money out. However, historical record proves, that it was the best buy people could ever get in stock market.

Buying assets in a falling market is less risky as compared to the times when prices have sky rocketed. **The Art of the deal is to buy as low as possible and take benefit of the market fluctuations. That is the safest risk and opportunity worth taking every time.**

UNDERSTAND INFLATION AND LET IT NOT MAKE YOU POOR

You might think that inflation and its effects on your money are very obvious. Everyone understands it and it doesn't need any more explanation or emphasis. Well, you are wrong! As they say, "Common Sense is not Common", so is the case with inflation. Many people don't understand inflation. And those who do are often unable to take it into account while making their financial or investment decisions. After all, why we would have billions of dollars stashed into current accounts or low yield bonds throughout the world? Why would we have so many people making hefty deposits in saving accounts which offer them income well below the annual inflation rate? Far worse is the situation in developing countries with large swaths of uneducated population. People hide cash for years and years hoping that they would become millionaires one day. That day never comes.

Inflation if simply put is something which erodes the purchasing power of your money. Every year we eagerly wait for a pay rise. But despite getting several pay rises, our lifestyle largely remains the same. That's because the goods we want to buy and services we want to hire get expensive every passing year. Yes it's the invisible ghost of Inflation which eats up your every pay rise. Now comes the question: How to avoid it?

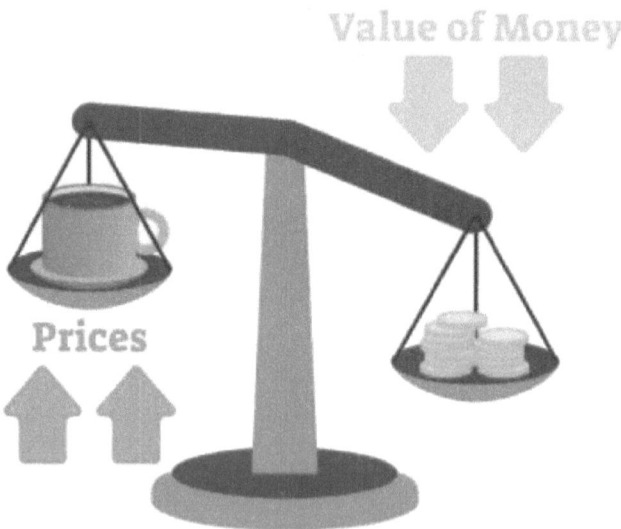

The key to protect your savings from inflation is to **invest them in assets that grow higher than inflation**. You must remain cognizant of current inflation rate (which will differ time to time and country to country) and invest your money in assets which have potential to produce higher yield than current inflation. But what exactly should be your investment strategy to beat the inflation and protect your savings?

One thing that you must always endeavour is to actively manage your passive investments. Sleeping on your invesments can give you significant profit but not the exlosive returns you can get if you remain abreast with market trends. Global changes, drastic market fluctuations, latest crypto currencies, best IPO offers, underdeveloped neghbourhood with a potential to rise in real estate value and a robust startup business your friend just started are oppurtunities for you to capitalize. Move your money and swing it from sector to sector, asset class to asset class. How you can actively manage your investment portfolio for big gains is explained in last two chapters of this book. But before you invest your money, you have to save some money? How you do it? I explain in next chapter.

THE MOST IMPORTANT KEY TO GETTING RICH IS TO CONTROL YOUR SPENDING

The *Money Gurus* tell us a simple three step formula of getting rich. It is:

Control your spending – Saving – Investing

The most important thing is to know the most importing thing. And that is what rich people don't tell us in this formula. That most important thing is to control your spending. Period.

Lot many people win millionaire lotteries and raffles throughout the world. How many of them are able to turn their million into millions or billion. Not because they didn't invest. It's because they didn't do the first thing right – which was to control their spending after getting instantaneously rich. Yes, they bought the fancy car and went on that expensive vacation they always dreamt of. A lot of the middle class fall into the same trap. When we get the pay rise, we increase our spending. This way we increase our spending instead of increasing our saving and continue to live from pay check to pay check.

Now you may argue that investing is more important than controlling your expenses. Why do I think otherwise?

Compare the billions of dollars which MNCs spent to market their consumer products than the paltry sum spent by banks and financial services companies to attract people. MNCs worldwide spend about 560 Billion US dollars on advertising. Some of these companies are richer than many countries. You just can't beat them. They study your needs, your strength, your weaknesses and your deep dark desires. The key to any business is its ability to fulfill the need of people. But the key to sophisticated business is to create the need itself. That's what they do. They 'make your need' and then fulfill it. They make you want what they have to offer. That's why we see long queues outside departmental stores and malls before Black Friday and New Year Sales but such scenes are
non-existent when it comes to banks, stock exchange, real estate and investment companies?

In our daily life, we spent numerous hours watching marketing and advertisement campaigns on television, internet, newspapers and billboards. Our screen time on TV, computer or cell phone is increasing and so is this addiction of consumerism. We must understand that MNCs play with our psychology and we end up buying things which we don't need and that's why shouldn't stretch ourselves to 'afford'.

As I explained earlier in the chapter Don't try to look rich, our quest for appearing wealthy prevents us from controlling our spending. Quite often, the middle class is inspired by the lavish lifestyle of rich people. So they imitate them by buying the same brands that they use and feel rich. What they don't realize is that expenditure of rich people on their lifestyle is paltry sum of their wealth. But in case of middle class, it is significant.

So remember that the most important key to build wealth is *to control your spending.*

YOUR INVESTMENT STRATEGY

Let it be very simple at the outset. Your investment strategy at any given time **should be able to beat the inflation and must produce a higher yield than being offered by saving accounts, bonds and Insurance policies**. Don't follow the advice of *Money Gurus* if they tell you otherwise. It is usually our 'safe play mindset' further exacerbated by clever marketing of Banks and Insurance Companies which takes us away from all so called 'riskier' investment avenues. The 'Assured Profit' offered by Banks and Insurance companies tricks us into opting for lowest wealth growing methods. If we analyze closely, risk is **'fear of capital loss in an Investor's mind'**. It is this fear which is exploited to lure investor towards guaranteed profit instruments. But if you see the historical data of last 150 years of stocks and commodities investments, a capital doesn't lose capital if he can hold his investments for an appropriate time. Instead, he is able to make better gains than Banks and Insurance companies. Avoiding Insurance Companies doesn't mean that you should not opt for Business or Car Insurance as well. What you should avoid is zero risk term based policies that Insurance Companies offer.

Another investment avenue that you can opt for is Real Estate. One of the key benefits of Real Estate is its protection against market risk. If held for appropriate duration, Real Estate always rises in value. But return on investment in Real Estate varies drastically depending upon time, type and location. Moment you buy Real Estate is critical. At times an upsurge comes and property booms. That is surely not the good time to buy. As I will explain later, if one wants to make money, then timing your deal to buy an asset below its actual value is of utmost importance. Secondly, Real Estate has different types such as commercial, residential, land or rental property. All these types have different risk and rewards. Last but definitely not the least, the location. Location of Real Estate is one of the most important factors and often determines its value. From which city you are choosing to buy Real Estate asset in to which corner of the street your property lies, location remains the critical factor.

Investing in crypto currencies could be another option. During the initial years of crypto currencies, they made explosive gains and drew everyone's attention but depreciated drastically when governments started banning these currencies. However, despite finacial and legal curbs around crypto currencies, they have managed to survive and still hold attraction of many, especially millineals. Crytpo currencies is a high risk high reward proposition. Because of uncerainty around future of crypto currencies vis a vis their growth potential amidst continued debasement of US Dollar, you should put as much money in crytpo as you can afford to lose.

Another place where you can invest is startup businesses. Although your investment in a successful startup business can often give highest Return on Investment (ROI), you must only commit your investment after thorough study of the business model and having developed a trustworthy relationship with your active partner. Table below summarizes the investment avenues that you should and should not choose:

Where you should not invest	*Where you should invest*
Saving Accounts	Stock Market
Term Based Insurance Policies	Mutual Funds(Must Reinvest bigger part of your dividends)
Bonds	Real Estate
	Startup Business Financing
	Commodity Trading(Gold, Oil etc.)

So If you want to be an active Investor who want to build his wealth fast, adopt an investment strategy which always beats the existing inflation and is able to offer more profit than risk

free assets such as bonds, saving accounts and Insurance policies.

SECTOR SWING – BEST STRATEGY FOR BUILDING UP YOUR WEALTH

Majority of the people are not able to grow their investment fast enough to become rich. It is because their investment either remain stagnant in one sector for a time longer than desired or divided in various sectors as a diversified portfolio. They think that they are doing the' right thing'. It is not their fault as they are constantly bombarded and are duped by *Money Gurus* who instill them with fear of capital loss and going broke if they don't follow their advice. In order to dupe gullible folks, *Money Gurus* use the two so called timeless investment strategies which I call **'Investment Fallacies'**. These fallacies are also peddled by financial companies and main stream media.

The first fallacy is 'Long Term Investment'. For an investor who has major investment in one sector let's say equity, he is told by likes of Warren Buffet to 'Stay invested' even before impending market crashes and 'Invest in Stocks with a belief that it will open after ten or twenty years'. The people who own real estate are told to never sell their property as it always grows in value. Same is the case for people with investment in precious metals such as Gold or Silver (Remember the proverb: '*Gold Never Loses its Glitter*').

Then we find 'finance specialists' instructing people to diversify their portfolio as best risk aversion strategy. I call this 'Diversification Fallacy'. In this, the *Money Gurus* want you to diversify your wealth in different sectors such as stocks, mutual funds, bonds, Gold ETFs, real estate etc. Logic is simple. If one or two sectors of your portfolio go down, others will grow in value and make up for the loss thus preserving your capital. By portfolio investment you also reap benefits of growth in different sectors and achieve handsome overall growth of your capital.

Now you may argue that If the human experience of recorded history suggests that long term investment achieves best compounding effect and diversified portfolio mitigates an investor's risk, why then should the both strategies, be called 'Fallacies'?

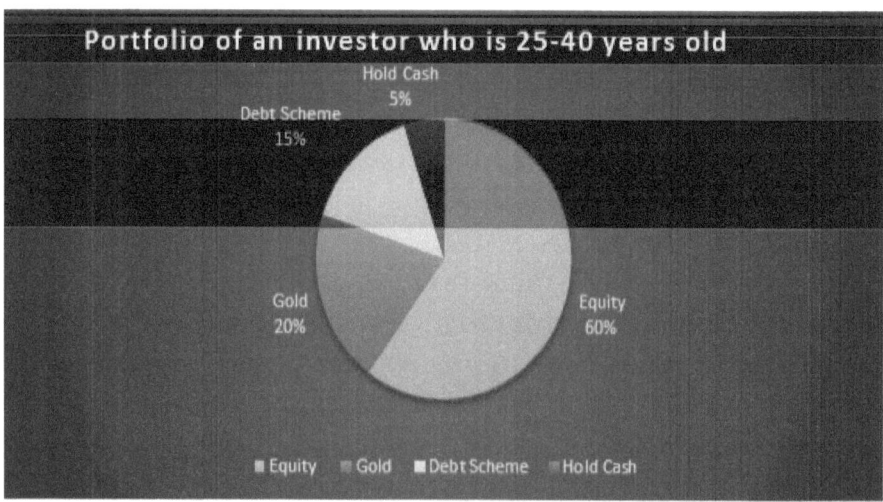

Answer is simple, I consider long term investment and portfolio diversification as good risk aversion strategies (Remember hearing suggestions like, Never take a loss, Don't sell cheap, Our favorite holding period is forever, Don't put all your eggs in one basket). But they aren't the best strategies of growing your wealth fast. These strategies don't have that 'multiplying effect' which you yearn for. Instead you are 'advised' to grow old with your investments and get rich before moving to a Care Home! Is that the ultimate success? To be rich with rheumatoid arthritis?

We must understand that markets move and fluctuate in cycles. Common people who have basic financial knowledge and keep a good watch over market, can join the upward. However, among these people, very few are able to join the initial rally. It is in these rallies or stack market booms where actual profit is made. It is important to note that rallies generally occur after drastic market crashes or Bloodbaths! At this time, which is just before start of the rally, conservative investor has either left the market already or is too fearful to enter. Smart investors are those who are in the market before the start of major moves. However, as indicated earlier, these smart investors are small in number. The majority follows suit towards the middle or end of a big move when rally has lost most of its steam. That's how many of us miss the opportunity to make big gains.

The best strategy to build your wealth fast is what I call sector swing. It is swing trade which is not bound to one particular sector, such as stocks, bonds, commodities or real estate. It is highest risk (which you can reduce by research) highest return approach where instead of opting for a diversified portfolio, you will shift your all capital from the one you have already invested in to the one with highest profit potential.

Take this example. If in 1970, if a person, let's say, Steve, had thoroughly researched the commodity market, and found investment potential in gold. If Steve, considering the obvious indicators like prevailing oil crises, hyperinflation, weaker USD and political uncertainty, had converted his investments in stocks and real estate into gold, he would have turned himself a millionaire by 1980. By 1980, this man who did his research, did not opt for a diversified portfolio like his 'well-advised' risk averse peers, and made timely entry in yellow metal market, would have turned his, let's say, USD 20000$ into staggering USD 4.8 Million within a decade. That's an increase by 2300%. Same is the story for those who bought Apple IPO in 1980 or purchased real estate in Manhattan New York in 1990s.

If you want to build your wealth exponentially and you want to do it fast, adopt Sector Swing Strategy (SSS). SSS has four simple steps:

- Do your research (Better you do lesser risk you take)

- Liquidate your investments (Get rid of diversified portfolio)

- Invest in the sector you have researched for

- Be patient and hold your investment till substantial return (You should hold till you believe that the current investment sector is best for optimum growth)

AFTERWORD

Like many of you, I have come accross thousands of youtube videos, blogs, articles and books on investments and getting rich. Obviously, the appeal of being wealthy is so strong that we are inadvertently attracted towards reading and watching money related stuff. Yet, many of us fail to multiply our investments and end up living pay check to pay check. What are we missing? Why are we failing?

This book was written after personal experience of having tried so many money tips available for free. There is so much we need to ignore, refute and dismiss when it comes to money. This book was written to de-clutter the noise around money making tips and bust some common myths.

ABOUT THE AUTHOR

Peter Pen

A freelance author, essayst, colunminst and satirist.

.